D0519155

THE ILLUSTRATED POETS

Shakespeare's Love Sonnets

EDITED BY
Daniel Burnstone

This edition first published by Parragon Books Ltd in 1995

Produced by
Magpie Books Ltd, 7 Kensington Church Court
London W8 4SP

Cover Picture: *The Young Lovers* by Gerard Hoet, Haynes
Fine Art at the Bindery Galleries, Broadway/Bridgeman
Art Library. Illustrations courtesy of: Mary Evans Picture
Library; Christies Images.

ISBN 0 75250 036 8

A copy of the British Library Cataloguing in Publication
Data is available from the British Library.

Typeset by Hewer Text Composition Services, Edinburgh
Printed in Singapore by Printlink International Co.

THE ILLUSTRATED POETS
SHAKESPEARE'S LOVE SONNETS

Sonnet 17

Who will believe my verse in time to come,
If it were fill'd with your most high deserts?
Though yet, heaven knows, it is but as a tomb
Which hides your life and shows not half your
    parts.
If I could write the beauty of your eyes
And in fresh numbers number all your graces,
The age to come would say 'This poet lies;
Such heavenly touches ne'er touch'd earthly
    faces.'
So should my papers yellow'd with their age
Be scorn'd like old men of less truth than
    tongue,
And your true rights be term'd a poet's rage
And stretched metre of an antique song:
    But were some child of yours alive that time,
    You should live twice, in it and in my rime.

Sonnet 18

Shall I compare thee to a summer's day?
Thou art more lovely and more temperate:
Rough winds do shake the darling buds of
      May,
And summer's lease hath all too short a date:
Sometime too hot the eye of heaven shines,
And often is his gold complexion dimm'd;
And every fair from fair sometime declines
By chance or nature's changing course
      untrimm'd;
But thy eternal summer shall not fade
Nor lose possession of that fair thou ow'st;
Nor shall Death brag thou wander'st in his
      shade,
When in eternal lines to time thou grow'st:
  So long as men can breathe or eyes can
      see,
  So long lives this and this gives life to thee.

Sonnet 19

Devouring Time, blunt thou the lion's paws,
And make the earth devour her own sweet
        brood;
Pluck the keen teeth from the fierce tiger's jaws,
And burn the long-lived phoenix in her blood;
Make glad and sorry seasons as thou fleets,
And do whate'er thou wilt, swift-footed Time,
To the wide world and all her fading sweets;
But I forbid thee one most heinous crime:
O, carve not with thy hours my love's fair brow,
Nor draw no lines there with thine antique pen;
Him in thy course untainted do allow
For beauty's pattern to succeeding men.
    Yet, do thy worst, old Time: despite thy
        wrong,
    My love shall in my verse ever live young.

Sonnet 20

A woman's face with Nature's own hand painted
Hast thou, the master-mistress of my passion;
A woman's gentle heart, but not acquainted
With shifting change, as is false women's
        fashion;
An eye more bright than theirs, less false in
        rolling,
Gilding the object whereupon it gazeth;
A man in hue, all hues in his controlling,
Which steals men's eyes and women's souls
        amazeth.
And for a woman wert thou first created;
Till Nature, as she wrought thee, fell a-doting,
And by addition me of thee defeated,
By adding one thing to my purpose nothing.
    But since she prick'd thee out for women's
        pleasure,
    Mine be thy love and thy love's use their
        treasure.

Sonnet 22

My glass shall not persuade me I am old,
So long as youth and thou are of one date;
But when in thee time's furrows I behold,
Then look I death my days should expiate.
For all that beauty that doth cover thee
Is but the seemly raiment of my heart,
Which in thy breast doth live as thine in me:
How can I then be elder than thou art?
O therefore, love, be of thyself so wary
As I, not for myself but for thee, will;
Bearing thy heart, which I will keep so chary
As tender nurse her babe from faring ill.

    Presume not on thy heart when mine is
       slain;
    Thou gavest me thine, not to give back
       again.

Sonnet 23

As an unperfect actor on the stage
Who with his fear is put beside his part,
Or some fierce thing replete with too much
rage,
Whose strength's abundance weakens his own
heart,
So I, for fear of trust, forget to say
The perfect ceremony of love's rite,
And in mine own love's strength seem to decay,
O'ercharged with burden of mine own love's
might.
O, let my looks be then the eloquence
And dumb presagers of my speaking breast;
Who plead for love and look for recompense
More than that tongue that more hath more
express'd.

O, learn to read what silent love hath writ:
To hear with eyes belongs to love's fine wit.

Sonnet 24

Mine eye hath play'd the painter and hath stell'd
Thy beauty's form in table of my heart;
My body is the frame wherein 't is held,
And pérspective it is best painter's art.
For through the painter must you see his skill,
To find where your true image pictured lies;
Which in my bosom's shop is hanging still,
That hath his windows glazed with thine eyes.
Now see what good turns eyes for eyes have
    done:
Mine eyes have drawn thy shape, and thine for
    me
Are windows to my breast, where-through the
    sun
Delights to peep, to gaze therein on thee;
    Yet eyes this cunning want to grace their art,
    They draw but what they see, know not the
        heart.

Sonnet 26

Lord of my love, to whom in vassalage
Thy merit hath my duty strongly knit,
To thee I send this written ambassage,
To witness duty, not to show my wit:
Duty so great, which wit so poor as mine
May make seem bare, in wanting words to
show it,
But that I hope some good conceit of thine
In thy soul's thought, all naked, will bestow
it;
Till whatsoever star that guides my moving
Points on me graciously with fair aspect
And puts apparel on my tatter'd loving,
To show me worthy of thy sweet respect:
Then may I dare to boast how I do love
thee;
Till then not show my head where thou
mayst prove me.

Sonnet 27

Weary with toil, I haste me to my bed,
The dear repose for limbs with travel tired;
But then begins a journey in my head,
To work my mind, when body's work's
      expired:
For then my thoughts, from far where I
      abide,
Intend a zealous pilgrimage to thee,
And keep my drooping eyelids open wide,
Looking on darkness which the blind do see:
Save that my soul's imaginary sight
Presents thy shadow to my sightless view,
Which, like a jewel hung in ghastly night,
Makes black night beauteous and her old
      face new.
   Lo! thus, by day my limbs, by night my
      mind,
   For thee and for myself no quiet find.

Sonnet 28

How can I then return in happy plight,
That am debarr'd the benefit of rest?
When day's oppression is not eased by night,
But day by night, and night by day, oppress'd?
And each, though enemies to either's reign,
Do in consent shake hands to torture me;
The one by toil, the other to complain
How far I toil, still farther off from thee.
I tell the day, to please him, thou art bright,
And dost him grace when clouds do blot the
              heaven:
So flatter I the swart-complexion'd night;
When sparkling stars twire not thou gild'st the
              even.
    But day doth daily draw my sorrows longer,
    And night doth nightly make grief's strength
              seem stronger.

Sonnet 29

When, in disgrace with fortune and men's eyes,
I all alone beweep my outcast state,
And trouble deaf heaven with my bootless cries,
And look upon myself and curse my fate,
Wishing me like to one more rich in hope,
Featured like him, like him with friends
        possess'd,
Desiring this man's art and that man's scope,
With what I most enjoy contented least;
Yet in these thoughts myself almost despising,
Haply I think on thee, and then my state,
Like to the lark at break of day arising
From sullen earth, sings hymns at heaven's gate;
    For thy sweet love remember'd such wealth
        brings
    That then I scorn to change my state with
        kings.

Sonnet 30

When to the sessions of sweet silent thought
I summon up remembrance of things past,
I sigh the lack of many a thing I sought,
And with old woes new wail my dear time's
        waste:
Then can I drown an eye, unused to flow,
For precious friends hid in death's dateless night,
And weep afresh love's long since cancell'd
        woe,
And moan the expense of many a vanish'd sight:
Then can I grieve at grievances foregone,
And heavily from woe to woe tell o'er
The sad account of fore-bemoaned moan,
Which I new pay as if not paid before.
   But if the while I think on thee, dear friend,
   All losses are restored and sorrows end.

Sonnet 33

Full many a glorious morning have I seen
Flatter the mountain-tops with sovereign
   eye,
Kissing with golden face the meadows green,
Gilding pale streams with heavenly alchemy;
Anon permit the basest clouds to ride
With ugly rack on his celestial face,
And from the forlorn world his visage hide,
Stealing unseen to west with this disgrace:
Even so my sun one early morn did shine
With all-triumphant splendour on my brow;
But, out alack! he was but one hour mine,
The region cloud hath mask'd him from me
   now.
 Yet him for this my love no whit
   disdaineth;
 Suns of the world may stain when
   heaven's sun staineth.

Venus and Adonis, Jacopo Amigoni

Sonnet 34

Why didst thou promise such a beauteous
       day,
And make me travel forth without my cloak,
To let base clouds o'ertake me in my way,
Hiding thy bravery in their rotten smoke?
'T is not enough that through the cloud thou
       break,
To dry the rain on my storm-beaten face,
For no man well of such a salve can speak
That heals the wound and cures not the
       disgrace:
Nor can thy shame give physic to my grief;
Though thou repent, yet I have still the loss:
The offender's sorrow lends but weak relief
To him that bears the strong offence's cross.
    Ah! but those tears are pearl which thy
       love sheds,
    And they are rich and ransom all ill deeds.

Sonnet 35

No more be grieved at that which thou hast
      done:
Roses have thorns, and silver fountains mud;
Clouds and eclipses stain both moon and
      sun,
And loathsome canker lives in sweetest bud.
All men make faults, and even I in this,
Authórizing thy trespass with compare,
Myself corrupting, salving thy amiss,
Excusing thy sins more than thy sins are;
For to thy sensual fault I bring in sense –
Thy adverse party is thy advocate –
And 'gainst myself a lawful plea commence:
Such civil war is in my love and hate,

    That I an accessary needs must be
    To that sweet thief which sourly robs
       from me.

Sonnet 36

Let me confess that we two must be twain,
Although our undivided loves are one:
So shall those blots that do with me remain
Without thy help by me be borne alone.
In our two loves there is but one respect,
Though in our lives a separable spite,
Which though it alter not love's sole effect,
Yet doth it steal sweet hours from love's
                delight.
I may not evermore acknowledge thee,
Lest my bewailed guilt should do thee
                shame,
Nor thou with public kindness honour me,
Unless thou take that honour from thy
                name:
  But do not so; I love thee in such sort
  As, thou being mine, mine is thy good
                report.

Sonnet 37

As a decrepit father takes delight
To see his active child do deeds of youth,
So I, made lame by fortune's dearest spite,
Take all my comfort of thy worth and truth.
For whether beauty, birth, or wealth, or wit,
Or any of these all, or all, or more,
Entitled in thy parts do crowned sit,
I make my love engrafted to this store:
So then I am not lame, poor, nor despised,
Whilst that this shadow doth such substance
    give
That I in thy abundance am sufficed
And by a part of all thy glory live.
    Look, what is best, that best I wish in thee:
    This wish I have; then ten times happy
        me!

How can my Muse want subject to invent,
While thou dost breathe . . . ?

Sonnet 38

How can my Muse want subject to invent,
While thou dost breathe, that pour'st into
my verse
Thine own sweet argument, too excellent
For every vulgar paper to rehearse?
O, give thyself the thanks, if aught in me
Worthy perusal stand against thy sight;
For who's so dumb that cannot write to thee,
When thou thyself dost give invention light?
Be thou the tenth Muse, ten times more in
worth
Than those old nine which rimers invocate;
And he that calls on thee, let him bring forth
Eternal numbers to outlive long date.
    If my slight Muse do please these curious
    days,
    The pain be mine, but thine shall be the
    praise.

Sonnet 40

Take all my loves, my love, yea, take them all;
What hast thou then more than thou hadst
        before?
No love, my love, that thou mayst true love call;
All mine was thine before thou hadst this more.
Then if for my love thou my love receivest,
I cannot blame thee for my love thou usest;
But yet be blamed, if thou thyself deceivest
By wilful taste of what thyself refusest.
I do forgive thy robbery, gentle thief,
Although thou steal thee all my poverty;
And yet, love knows it is a greater grief
To bear love's wrong than hate's known injury.
    Lascivious grace, in whom all ill well shows,
    Kill me with spites; yet we must not be foes.

Love and Time, John Melhuish Strudwick

Sonnet 41

Those pretty wrongs that liberty commits,
When I am sometime absent from thy heart,
Thy beauty and thy years full well befits,
For still temptation follows where thou art.
Gentle thou art and therefore to be won,
Beauteous thou art, therefore to be assailed;
And when a woman woos, what woman's
     son
Will sourly leave her till she have prevailed?
Ay me! but yet thou mightst my seat forbear,
And chide thy beauty and thy straying youth,
Who lead thee in their riot even there
Where thou art forced to break a twofold
     truth,
  Hers, by thy beauty tempting her to thee,
  Thine, by thy beauty being false to me.

Sonnet 42

That thou hast her, it is not all my grief,
And yet it may be said I loved her dearly;
That she hath thee, is of my wailing chief,
A loss in love that touches me more nearly.
Loving offenders, thus I will excuse ye:
Thou dost love her, because thou know'st I love
        her;
And for my sake even so doth she abuse me,
Suffering my friend for my sake to approve her.
If I lose thee, my loss is my love's gain,
And losing her, my friend hath found that loss;
Both find each other, and I lose both twain,
And both for my sake lay on me this cross:
   But here's the joy; my friend and I are one;
   Sweet flattery! then she loves but me alone.

Sonnet 43

When most I wink, then do mine eyes best see,
For all the day they view things unrespected;
But when I sleep, in dreams they look on thee,
And darkly bright are bright in dark directed.
Then thou, whose shadow shadows doth make
       bright,
How would thy shadow's form form happy
       show
To the clear day with thy much clearer light,
When to unseeing eyes thy shade shines so!
How would, I say, mine eyes be blessed made
By looking on thee in the living day,
When in dead night thy fair imperfect shade
Through heavy sleep on sightless eyes doth stay!
  All days are nights to see till I see thee,
    And nights bright days when dreams do show
      thee me.

Sonnet 44

If the dull substance of my flesh were thought,
Injurious distance should not stop my way;
For then despite of space I would be brought,
From limits far remote, where thou dost stay.
No matter then although my foot did stand
Upon the farthest earth removed from thee;
For nimble thought can jump both sea and land
As soon as think the place where he would be.
But, ah! thought kills me that I am not thought,
To leap large lengths of miles when thou art
    gone,
But that, so much of earth and water wrought,
I must attend time's leisure with my moan,
   Receiving nought by elements so slow
   But heavy tears, badges of either's woe.

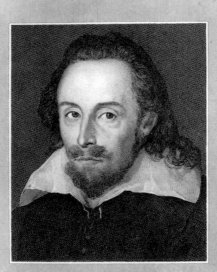

WM. SHAKSPEARE.

William Shakespeare

Sonnet 45

The other two, slight air and purging fire,
Are both with thee, wherever I abide;
The first my thought, the other my desire,
These present-absent with swift motion slide.
For when these quicker elements are gone
In tender embassy of love to thee,
My life, being made of four, with two alone
Sinks down to death, oppress'd with
      melancholy;
Until life's composition be recured
By those swift messengers return'd from thee,
Who even but now come back again, assured
Of thy fair health, recounting it to me:
  This told, I joy; but then no longer glad,
  I send them back again and straight grow sad.

Sonnet 46

Mine eye and heart are at a mortal war
How to divide the conquest of thy sight;
Mine eye my heart thy picture's sight would bar,
My heart mine eye the freedom of that right.
My heart doth plead that thou in him dost lie,
A closet never pierced with crystal eyes,
But the defendant doth that plea deny,
And says in him thy fair appearance lies.
To 'cide this title is impanneled
A quest of thoughts, all tenants to the heart;
And by their verdict is determined
The clear eye's moiety and the dear heart's part:
   As thus; mine eye's due is thy outward part,
   And my heart's right thy inward love of heart.

Being your slave, what should I do but tend
Upon the hours and times of your desire?

Sonnet 53

What is your substance, whereof are you
        made,
That millions of strange shadows on you
        tend?
Since every one hath, every one, one shade,
And you, but one, can every shadow lend.
Describe Adonis, and the counterfeit
Is poorly imitated after you;
On Helen's cheek all art of beauty set,
And you in Grecian tires are painted new:
Speak of the spring and foison of the year;
The one doth shadow of your beauty show,
The other as your bounty doth appear;
And you in every blessed shape we know.
   In all external grace you have some part,
   But you like none, none you, for constant
        heart.

Sonnet 54

O, how much more doth beauty beauteous
      seem
By that sweet ornament which truth doth give!
The rose looks fair, but fairer we it deem
For that sweet odour which doth in it live.
The canker-blooms have full as deep a dye
As the perfumed tincture of the roses,
Hang on such thorns and play as wantonly
When summer's breath their masked buds
      discloses:
But, for their virtue only is their show,
They live unwoo'd and unrespected fade,
Die to themselves. Sweet roses do not so;
Of their sweet deaths are sweetest odours made:
    And so of you, beauteous and lovely youth,
    When that shall fade, my verse distils your
      truth.

Sonnet 55

Not marble, nor the gilded monuments
Of princes, shall outlive this powerful rime;
But you shall shine more bright in these
          contents
Than unswept stone besmear'd with sluttish
          time.
When wasteful war shall statues overturn,
And broils root out the work of masonry,
Nor Mars his sword nor war's quick fire shall
          burn
The living record of your memory.
'Gainst death and all-oblivious enmity
Shall you pace forth: your praise shall still find
          room
Even in the eyes of all posterity
That wear this world out to the ending doom.
  So, till the judgement that yourself arise,
    You live in this, and dwell in lovers' eyes.

Sonnet 57

Being your slave, what should I do but tend
Upon the hours and times of your desire?
I have no precious time at all to spend,
Nor services to do, till you require.
Nor dare I chide the world-without-end hour
Whilst I, my sovereign, watch the clock for you,
Nor think the bitterness of absence sour
When you have bid your servant once adieu;
Nor dare I question with my jealous thought
Where you may be, or your affairs suppose,
But, like a sad slave, stay and think of nought
Save, where you are how happy you make
those.
  So true a fool is love that in your will,
  Though you do any thing, he thinks no ill.

Flirting, Richard Doyle

Sonnet 58

That god forbid that made me first your
        slave,
I should in thought control your times of
        pleasure,
Or at your hand the account of hours to
        crave,
Being your vassal, bound to stay your leisure!
O, let me suffer, being at your beck,
The imprison'd absence of your liberty;
And patience, tame to sufferance, bide each
        check,
Without accusing you of injury.
Be where you list, your charter is so strong
That you yourself may privilege your time;
Do what you will; to you it doth belong
Yourself to pardon of self-doing crime.
  I am to wait, though waiting so be hell;
  Not blame your pleasure, be it ill or well.

Sonnet 61

Is it thy will thy image should keep open
My heavy eyelids to the weary night?
Dost thou desire my slumbers should be
      broken,
While shadows like to thee do mock my
      sight?
Is it thy spirit that thou send'st from thee
So far from home into my deeds to pry,
To find out shames and idle hours in me,
The scope and tenour of thy jealousy?
O, no! thy love, though much, is not so
      great:
It is my love that keeps mine eye awake;
Mine own true love that doth my rest defeat,
To play the watchman ever for thy sake:
  For thee watch I whilst thou dost wake
      elsewhere,
  From me far off, with others all too near.

So are you to my thoughts as food to life

Sonnet 62

Sin of self-love possesseth all mine eye
And all my soul and all my every part;
And for this sin there is no remedy,
It is so grounded inward in my heart.
Methinks no face so gracious is as mine,
No shape so true, no truth of such account;
And for myself mine own worth do define,
As I all other in all worths surmount.
But when my glass shows me myself indeed,
Beated and chopp'd with tann'd antiquity,
Mine own self-love quite contrary I read;
Self so self-loving were iniquity.
   'Tis thee, myself, that for myself I praise,
    Painting my age with beauty of thy days.

Sonnet 73

That time of year thou mayst in me behold
When yellow leaves, or none, or few, do hang
Upon those boughs which shake against the
cold,
Bare ruin'd choirs where late the sweet birds
sang.
In me thou see'st the twilight of such day
As after sunset fadeth in the west;
Which by and by black night doth take away,
Death's second self, that seals up all in rest.
In me thou see'st the glowing of such fire
That on the ashes of his youth doth lie,
As the death-bed whereon it must expire,
Consumed with that which it was nourish'd by.
  This thou perceiv'st, which makes thy love
    more strong,
  To love that well which thou must leave ere
    long.

Sonnet 75

So are you to my thoughts as food to life,
Or as sweet-season'd showers are to the
        ground;
And for the peace of you I hold such strife
As 'twixt a miser and his wealth is found;
Now proud as an enjoyer and anon
Doubting the filching age will steal his
        treasure,
Now counting best to be with you alone,
Then better'd that the world may see my
        pleasure:
Sometime all full with feasting on your sight,
And by and by clean starved for a look;
Possessing or pursuing no delight,
Save what is had or must from you be took.
  Thus do I pine and surfeit day by day,
  Or gluttoning on all, or all away.

Sonnet 76

Why is my verse so barren of new pride,
So far from variation or quick change?
Why with the time do I not glance aside
To new-found methods and to compounds
       strange?
Why write I still all one, ever the same,
And keep invention in a noted weed,
That every word doth almost tell my name,
Showing their birth and where they did
       proceed?
O know, sweet love, I always write of you,
And you and love are still my argument;
So all my best is dressing old words new,
Spending again what is already spent:
  For as the sun is daily new and old,
  So is my love still telling what is told.

Shakespeare's birthplace

Sonnet 88

When thou shalt be disposed to set me light
And place my merit in the eye of scorn,
Upon thy side against myself I'll fight,
And prove thee virtuous, though thou art
     forsworn.
With mine own weakness being best
     acquainted,
Upon thy part I can set down a story
Of faults conceal'd, wherein I am attainted;
That thou in losing me shalt win much glory:
And I by this will be a gainer too;
For bending all my loving thoughts on thee,
The injuries that to myself I do,
Doing thee vantage, double-vantage me.
  Such is my love, to thee I so belong,
  That for thy right myself will bear all
     wrong.

Sonnet 90

Then hate me when thou wilt; if ever, now;
Now, while the world is bent my deeds to cross,
Join with the spite of fortune, make me bow,
And do not drop in for an after-loss:
Ah, do not, when my heart hath 'scaped this
    sorrow,
Come in the rearward of a conquer'd woe;
Give not a windy night a rainy morrow,
To linger out a purposed overthrow.
If thou wilt leave me, do not leave me last,
When other petty griefs have done their spite,
But in the onset come: so shall I taste
At first the very worst of fortune's might,
    And other strains of woe, which now seem
      woe,
    Compared with loss of thee will not seem so.

O, in what sweets dost thou thy sins enclose!

Sonnet 91

Some glory in their birth, some in their skill,
some in their wealth, some in their bodies'
       force;
Some in their garments, though new-fangled ill;
Some in their hawks and hounds, some in their
       horse;
And every humour hath his adjunct pleasure,
Wherein it finds a joy above the rest:
But these particulars are not my measure;
All these I better in one general best.
Thy love is better than high birth to me,
Richer than wealth, prouder than garments'
       cost,
Of more delight than hawks or horses be;
And having thee, of all men's pride I boast:
  Wretched in this alone, that thou mayst take
  All this away and me most wretched make.

Sonnet 93

So shall I live supposing thou art true,
Like a deceived husband; so love's face
May still seem love to me, though alter'd new;
Thy looks with me, thy heart in other place:
For there can live no hatred in thine eye,
Therefore in that I cannot know thy change.
In many's looks the false heart's history
Is writ in moods and frowns and wrinkles
                    strange.
But heaven in thy creation did decree
That in thy face sweet love should ever dwell;
Whate'er thy thoughts or thy heart's workings
                    be,
Thy looks should nothing thence but sweetness
                    tell.
    How like Eve's apple doth thy beauty grow,
    If thy sweet virtue answer not thy show!

Sonnet 94

They that have power to hurt and will do none,
That do not do the thing they most do show,
Who, moving others, are themselves as stone,
Unmoved, cold, and to temptation slow;
They rightly do inherit heaven's graces
And husband nature's riches from expense;
They are the lords and owners of their faces,
Others but stewards of their excellence.
The summer's flower is to the summer sweet,
Though to itself it only live and die,
But if that flower with base infection meet,
The basest weed outbraves his dignity:
  For sweetest things turn sourest by their
      deeds;
  Lilies that fester smell far worse than weeds.

Sonnet 95

How sweet and lovely dost thou make the
shame
Which, like a canker in the fragrant rose,
Doth spot the beauty of thy budding name!
O, in what sweets dost thou thy sins enclose!
That tongue that tells the story of thy days,
Making lascivious comments on thy sport,
Cannot dispraise but in a kind of praise;
Naming thy name blesses an ill report.
O, what a mansion have those vices got
Which for their habitation chose out thee,
Where beauty's veil doth cover every blot,
And all things turns to fair that eyes can see!
　　Take heed, dear heart, of this large
privilege;
　　The hardest knife ill-used doth lose his
edge.

For well thou know'st to my dear doting heart
Thou art the fairest and most precious jewel

Sonnet 97

How like a winter hath my absence been
From thee, the pleasure of the fleeting year!
What freezings have I felt, what dark days
seen!
What old December's bareness everywhere!
And yet this time remov'd was summer's
time;
The teeming autumn big with rich increase,
Bearing the wanton burthen of the prime,
Like widow'd wombs after their lords'
decease:
Yet this abundant issue seem'd to me
But hope of orphans and unfather'd fruit;
For summer and his pleasures wait on thee,
And, thou away, the very birds are mute;
    Or, if they sing, 't is with so dull a cheer
    That leaves look pale, dreading the
    winter's near.

Sonnet 110

Alas, 't is true I have gone here and there
And made myself a motley to the view,
Gored mine own thoughts, sold cheap what is
      most dear,
Made old offences of affections new;
Most true it is that I have look'd on truth
Askance and strangely: but, by all above,
These blenches gave my heart another youth,
And worse essays proved thee my best of love.
Now all is done, have what shall have no end:
Mine appetite I never more will grind
On newer proof, to try an older friend,
A god in love, to whom am confined.
    Then give me welcome, next my heaven the
      best,
    Even to thy pure and most most loving breast.

Cupid and Psyche, Jacopo Amigoni

Sonnet 115

Those lines that I before have writ do lie,
Even those that said I could not love you dearer:
Yet then my judgement knew no reason why
My most full flame should afterwards burn
    clearer.
But reckoning Time, whose million'd accidents
Creep in 'twixt vows and change decrees of
    kings,
Tan sacred beauty, blunt the sharp'st intents,
Divert strong minds to the course of altering
    things:-
Alas, why, fearing of Time's tyranny,
Might I not then say 'Now I love you best,'
When I was certain o'er incertainty,
Crowning the present, doubting of the rest?
   Love is a babe; then might I *not* say so,
    To give full growth to that which still doth
    grow.

Sonnet 116

Let me not to the marriage of true minds
Admit impediments. Love is not love
Which alters when it alteration finds,
Or bends with the remover to remove:
O, no! it is an ever-fixed mark,
That looks on tempests and is never shaken;
It is the star to every wandering bark,
Whose worth's unknown, although his
        height be taken.
Love's not Time's fool, though rosy lips and
        cheeks
Within his bending sickle's compass come;
Love alters not with his brief hours and
        weeks,
But bears it out even to the edge of doom.
  If this be error and upon me proved,
  I never writ, nor no man ever loved.

Sonnet 117

Accuse me thus: that I have scanted all
Wherein I should your great deserts repay;
Forgot upon your dearest love to call,
Whereto all bonds do tie me day by day;
That I have frequent been with unknown
minds,
And given to time your own dear-purchased
right;
That I have hoisted sail to all the winds
Which should transport me farthest from
your sight.
Book both my wilfulness and errors down,
And on just proof surmise accumulate;
Bring me within the level of your frown,
But shoot not at me in your waken'd hate;
Since my appeal says I did strive to prove
The constancy and virtue of your love.

Sonnet 124

If my dear love were but the child of state,
It might for Fortune's bastard be unfather'd,
As subject to Time's love or to Time's hate,
Weeds among weeds, or flowers with
        flowers gather'd.
No, it was builded far from accident;
It suffers not in smiling pomp, nor falls
Under the blow of thralled discontent,
Whereto the inviting time our fashion calls:
It fears not policy, that heretic,
Which works on leases of short-number'd
        hours,
But all alone stands hugely politic,
That it nor grows with heat nor drowns with
        showers.
    To this I witness call the fools of time,
    Which die for goodness, who have lived
        for crime.

The Fountain of Youth,
Charles Napier Kennedy

Sonnet 126

O thou, my lovely boy, who in thy power
Dost hold Time's fickle glass, his sickle-hour;
Who hast by waning grown, and therein
       show'st
Thy lovers withering as thy sweet self
       grow'st;
If Nature, sovereign mistress over wrack,
As thou goest onwards, still will pluck thee
       back,
She keeps thee to this purpose, that her skill
May time disgrace and wretched minutes
       kill.
Yet fear her, O thou minion of her pleasure!
She may detain, but not still keep, her
       treasure:
Her audit, though delay'd, answer'd must be,
And her quietus is to render thee.

Sonnet 127

In the old age black was not counted fair,
Or if it were, it bore not beauty's name;
But now is black beauty's successive heir,
And beauty slander'd with a bastard shame:
For since each hand hath put on nature's
        power,
Fairing the foul with art's false borrow'd face,
Sweet beauty hath no name, no holy bower,
But is profaned, if not lives in disgrace.
Therefore my mistress' brows are raven
        black,
Her eyes so suited, and they mourners seem
At such who, not born fair, no beauty lack,
Slandering creation with a false esteem:
   Yet so they mourn, becoming of their
       woe,
   That every tongue says beauty should
       look so.

Distant View of Stratford-on-Avon,
Francis S. Walker

Sonnet 128

How oft, when thou, my music, music play'st,
Upon that blessed wood whose motion sounds
With thy sweet fingers, when thou gently
      sway'st
The wiry concord that mine ear confounds,
Do I envy those jacks that nimble leap
To kiss the tender inward of thy hand,
Whilst my poor lips, which should that harvest
      reap,
At the wood's boldness by thee blushing stand!

To be so tickled, they would change their state
And situation with those dancing chips,
O'er whom thy fingers walk with gentle gait,
Making dead wood more blest than living lips.
  Since saucy jacks so happy are in this,
    Give them thy fingers, me thy lips to kiss.

Sonnet 129

The expense of spirit in a waste of shame
Is lust in action; and till action, lust
Is perjured, murderous, bloody, full of
      blame,
Savage, extreme, rude, cruel, not to trust;
Enjoy'd no sooner but despised straight;
Past reason hunted, and no sooner had,
Past reason hated, as a swallow'd bait
On purpose laid to make the taker mad:
Mad in pursuit and in possession so;
Had, having, and in quest to have, extreme;
A bliss in proof, and proved, a very woe;
Before a joy proposed; behind a dream.
    All this the world well knows; yet none
        knows well
    To shun the heaven that leads men to this
        hell.

Sonnet 130

My mistress' eyes are nothing like the sun;
Coral is far more red than her lips' red:
If snow be white, why then her breasts are dun;
If hairs be wires, black wires grow on her head.
I have seen roses damask'd, red and white,
But no such roses see I in her cheeks;

And in some perfumes is there more delight
Than in the breath that from my mistress reeks.
I love to hear her speak, yet well I know
That music hath a far more pleasing sound:
I grant I never saw a goddess go;
My mistress, when she walks, treads on the
        ground:
  And yet, by heaven, I think my love as rare
  As any she belied with false compare.

Sonnet 131

Thou art as tyrannous, so as thou art,
As those whose beauties proudly make them
       cruel;
For well thou know'st to my dear doting heart
Thou art the fairest and most precious jewel.
Yet in good faith some say that thee behold
Thy face hath not the power to make love
       groan:
To say they err I dare not be so bold,
Although I swear it to myself alone.
And, to be sure that is not false I swear,
A thousand groans, but thinking on thy face,
One on another's neck, do witness bear
Thy black is fairest in my judgement's place.
  In nothing art thou black save in thy deeds,
  And thence this slander, as I think, proceeds.

But when she saw my woeful state,
Straight in her heart did mercy come

Sonnet 132

Thine eyes I love, and they, as pitying me,
Knowing thy heart torments me with disdain,
Have put on black and loving mourners be,
Looking with pretty ruth upon my pain.
And truly not the morning sun of heaven
Better becomes the grey cheeks of the east,

Nor that full star that ushers in the even
Doth half that glory to the sober west,
As those two mourning eyes become thy face:
O, let it then as well beseem thy heart
To mourn for me, since mourning doth thee
        grace,
And suit thy pity like in every part.
  Then will I swear Beauty herself is black
  And all they foul that thy complexion lack.

Sonnet 133

Beshrew that heart that makes my heart to groan
For that deep wound it gives my friend and me!
Is 't not enough to torture me alone,
But slave to slavery my sweet'st friend must be?
Me from myself thy cruel eye hath taken,
And my next self thou harder hast engross'd:
Of him, myself, and thee, I am forsaken;
A torment thrice threefold thus to be cross'd.
Prison my heart in thy steel bosom's ward,
But then my friend's heart let my poor heart
      bail;
Whoe'er keeps me, let my heart be his guard;
Thou canst not then use rigour in my gaol:
    And yet thou wilt; for I, being pent in thee,
    Perforce am thine, and all that is in me.

God Speed, Edmund Blair Leighton

Sonnet 134

So, now I have confess'd that he is thine
And I myself am mortgaged to thy will,
Myself I'll forfeit, so that other mine
Thou wilt restore, to be my comfort still:
But thou wilt not, nor he will not be free,
For thou art covetous and he is kind;

He learn'd but surety-like to write for me,
Under that bond that him as fast doth bind.
The statute of thy beauty thou wilt take,
Thou usurer, that put'st forth all to use,
And sue a friend came debtor for my sake;
So him I lose through my unkind abuse.
   Him have I lost; thou hast both him and
     me:
   He pays the whole, and yet am I not free.

Sonnet 135

Whoever hath her wish, thou hast thy will,
And 'Will' to boot, and 'Will' in overplus;
More than enough am I that vex thee still,
To thy sweet will making addition thus.
Wilt thou, whose will is large and spacious,
Not once vouchsafe to hide my will in thine?
Shall will in others seem right gracious,
And in my will no fair acceptance shine?
The sea, all water, yet receives rain still
And in abundance addeth to his store;
So thou, being rich in will, add to thy will
One will of mine, to make thy large will
     more.
  Let no unkind no fair beseechers kill;
  Think all but one, and me in that one
     'Will.'

Sonnet 136

If thy soul check thee that I come so near,
Swear to thy blind soul that I was thy 'Will,'
And will, thy soul knows, is admitted there;
Thus far for love my love-suit, sweet, fulfil.
Will will fulfil the treasure of thy love,
Ay, fill it full with wills, and my will one.
In things of great receipt with ease we prove
Among a number one is reckon'd none:
Then in the number let me pass untold,
Though in thy store's account I one must be;
For nothing hold me, so it please thee hold
That nothing me, a something, sweet, to
       thee:
  Make but my name thy love, and love that
      still,
  And then thou lov'st me, for my name is
      'Will.'

Sonnet 137

Thou blind fool, Love, what dost thou to mine
eyes,
That they behold, and see not what they see?
They know what beauty is, see where it lies,
Yet what the best is take the worst to be.
If eyes corrupt by over-partial looks
Be anchor'd in the bay where all men ride,
Why of eyes' falsehood hast thou forged hooks,
Whereto the judgement of my heart is tied?
Why should my heart think that a several plot
Which my heart knows the wide world's
common place?
Or mine eyes seeing this, say this is not,
To put fair truth upon so foul a face?
  In things right true my heart and eyes have
  erred,
  And to this false plague are they now
  transferr'd.

Cupid Sharpening his Arrows, Francesco Gessi

Sonnet 138

When my love swears that she is made of
    truth
I do believe her, though I know she lies,
That she might think me some untutor'd
    youth,
Unlearned in the world's false subtleties.
Thus vainly thinking that she thinks me
    young,
Although she knows my days are past the
    best,
Simply I credit her false-speaking tongue:
On both sides thus is simple truth suppress'd.
But wherefore says she not she is unjust?
And wherefore say not I that I am old?
O, love's best habit is in seeming trust,
And age in love loves not to have years told:
    Therefore I lie with her and she with me,
    And in our faults by lies we flatter'd be.

Sonnet 139

O, call not me to justify the wrong
That thy unkindness lays upon my heart;
Wound me not with thine eye but with thy
        tongue;
Use power with power and slay me not by art.
Tell me thou lov'st elsewhere; but in my sight,
Dear heart, forbear to glance thine eye aside:
What need'st thou wound with cunning when
        thy might
Is more than my o'er-press'd defence can bide?
Let me excuse thee: ah! my love well knows
Her pretty looks have been mine enemies,
And therefore from my face she turns my foes,
That they elsewhere might dart their injuries:
   Yet do not so; but since I am near slain,
   Kill me outright with looks and rid my pain.

Sonnet 140

Be wise as thou art cruel; do not press
My tongue-tied patience with too much
                    disdain;
Lest sorrow lend me words and words
                    express
The manner of my pity-wanting pain.
If I might teach thee wit, better it were,
Though not to love, yet, love, to tell me so;
As testy sick men, when their deaths be near,
No news but health from their physicians
                    know;
For if I should despair, I should grow mad,
And in my madness might speak ill of thee:
Now this ill-wresting world is grown so bad,
Mad slanderers by mad ears believed be.
    That I may not be so, nor thou belied,
    Bear thine eyes straight, though thy proud
                    heart go wide.

Sonnet 141

In faith, I do not love thee with mine eyes,
For they in thee a thousand errors note;
But 't is my heart that loves what they
        despise,
Who in despite of view is pleased to dote;
Nor are mine ears with thy tongue's tune
        delighted;
Nor tender feeling to base touches prone,
Nor taste, nor smell, desire to be invited
To any sensual feast with thee alone:
But my five wits nor my five senses can
Dissuade one foolish heart from serving thee,
Who leaves unsway'd the likeness of a man,
Thy proud heart's slave and vassal wretch to
        be:
  Only my plague thus far I count my gain,
  That she that makes me sin awards me
        pain.

Sonnet 142

Love is my sin and thy dear virtue hate,
Hate of my sin, grounded on sinful loving:
O, but with mine compare thou thine own
state,
And thou shalt find it merits not reproving;
Or, if it do, not from those lips of thine,
That have profaned their scarlet ornaments
And seal'd false bonds of love as oft as mine,
Robb'd others' beds' revénues of their rents.
Be it lawful I love thee, as thou lov'st those
Whom thine eyes woo as mine impórtune
thee:
Root pity in thy heart, that when it grows
Thy pity may deserve to pitied be.
    If thou dost seek to have what thou dost
    hide,
    By self-example mayst thou be denied!

·

Sonnet 143

Lo! as a careful huswife runs to catch
One of her feather'd creatures broke away,
Sets down her babe, and makes all swift
        dispatch
In púrsuit of the thing she would have stay;
Whilst her neglected child holds her in
        chase,
Cries to catch her whose busy care is bent
To follow that which flies before her face,
Not prizing her poor infant's discontent:
So runn'st thou after that which flies from
        thee,
Whilst I thy babe chase thee afar behind;
But if thou catch thy hope, turn back to me,
And play the mother's part, kiss me, be kind:
    So will I pray that thou mayst have thy
        'Will,'
    If thou turn back, and my loud crying still.

Sonnet 144

Two loves I have, of comfort and despair,
Which like two spirits do suggest me still:
The better angel is a man right fair,
The worser spirit a woman colour'd ill.
To win me soon to hell, my female evil
Tempteth my better angel from my side,
And would corrupt my saint to be a devil,
Wooing his purity with her foul pride.

And whether that my angel be turn'd fiend
Suspect I may, yet not directly tell;
But being both from me, both to each friend,
I guess one angel in another's hell:
    Yet this shall I ne'er know, but live in
        doubt,
    Till my bad angel fire my good one out.

Sonnet 145

Those lips that Love's own hand did make
Breathed forth the sound that said 'I hate'
To me that languish'd for her sake;
But when she saw my woeful state,
Straight in her heart did mercy come,
Chiding that tongue that ever sweet
Was used in giving gentle doom,
And taught it thus anew to greet;
'I hate' she alter'd with an end,
That follow'd it as gentle day
Doth follow night, who like a fiend
From heaven to hell is flown away;
  'I hate' from hate away she threw,
    And saved my life, saying 'not you.'

Sonnet 147

My love is as a fever, longing still
For that which longer nurseth the disease;
Feeding on that which doth preserve the ill,
The uncertain sickly appetite to please.
My reason, the physician to my love,
Angry that his prescriptions are not kept,
Hath left me, and I desperate now approve
Desire is death, which physic did except.
Past cure I am, now reason is past care,
And frantic-mad with evermore unrest;
My thoughts and my discourse as madmen's
                    are,
At random from the truth vainly express'd;
    For I have sworn thee fair, and thought
                    thee bright,
    Who art as black as hell, as dark as night.

Sonnet 148

O me, what eyes hath Love put in my head,
Which have no correspondence with true sight!
Or, if they have, where is my judgement fled,
That censures falsely what they see aright?
If that be fair whereon my false eyes dote,
What means the world to say it is not so?
If it be not, then love doth well denote
Love's eye is not so true as all men's: No,
How can it? O, how can Love's eye be true,
That is so vex'd with watching and with tears?
No marvel then, though I mistake my view;
The sun itself sees not till heaven clears.
    O cunning Love! with tears thou keep'st me
        blind,
    Lest eyes well-seeing thy foul faults should
        find.

Sonnet 149

Canst thou, O cruel! say I love thee not,
When I against myself with thee partake?
Do I not think on thee, when I forgot
Am of myself, all-tyrant, for thy sake?
Who hateth thee that I do call my friend?
On whom frown'st thou that I do fawn
       upon?
Nay, if thou lour'st on me, do I not spend
Revenge upon myself with present moan?
What merit do I in myself respect,
That is so proud thy service to despise,
When all my best doth worship thy defect,
Commanded by the motion of thine eyes?
    But, love, hate on, for now I know thy
      mind;
    Those that can see thou lov'st, and I am
      blind.

Sonnet 150

O, from what power hast thou this powerful
           might
With insufficiency my heart to sway?
To make me give the lie to my true sight,
And swear that brightness doth not grace the
           day?
Whence hast thou this becoming of things ill,
That in the very refuse of thy deeds
There is such strength and warrantise of skill
That, in my mind, thy worst all best exceeds?
Who taught thee how to make me love thee
           more
The more I hear and see just cause of hate?
O, though I love what others do abhor,
With others thou shouldst not abhor my state:
    If thy unworthiness raised love in me,
    More worthy I to be beloved of thee.

Sonnet 151

Love is too young to know what conscience
    is;
Yet who knows not conscience is born of
    love?
Then, gentle cheater, urge not my amiss,
Lest guilty of my faults thy sweet self prove:
For, thou betraying me, I do betray
My nobler part to my gross body's treason;
My soul doth tell my body that he may
Triumph in love; flesh stays no farther
    reason,
But, rising at thy name, doth point out thee
As his triumphant prize. Proud of this pride,
He is contented thy poor drudge to be,
To stand in thy affairs, fall by thy side.
    No want of conscience hold it that I call
    Her 'love' for whose dear love I rise and
    fall.

Sonnet 152

In loving thee thou know'st I am forsworn,
But thou art twice forsworn, to me love
            swearing;
In act thy bed-vow broke and new faith torn
In vowing new hate after new love bearing.
But why of two oaths' breach do I accuse thee,
When I break twenty? I am perjured most;
For all my vows are oaths but to misuse thee,
And all my honest faith in thee is lost:
For I have sworn deep oaths of thy deep
            kindness,
Oaths of thy love, thy truth, thy constancy;
And, to enlighten thee, gave eyes to blindness,
Or made them swear against the thing they see;
    For I have sworn thee fair; more perjured I,
    To swear against the truth so foul a lie!

Sonnet 153

Cupid laid by his brand, and fell asleep:
A maid of Dian's this advantage found,
And his love-kindling fire did quickly steep
In a cold valley-fountain of that ground;
Which borrow'd from this holy fire of Love
A dateless lively heat, still to endure,
And grew a seething bath, which yet men prove
Against strange maladies a sovereign cure.
But at my mistress's eye Love's brand new-fired,
The boy for trial needs would touch my breast;
I, sick withal, the help of bath desired,
And thither hied, a sad distemper'd guest,
    But found no cure: the bath for my help lies
    Where Cupid got new fire – my mistress'
        eyes.

Sonnet 154

The little Love-god lying once asleep
Laid by his side his heart-inflaming brand,
Whilst many nymphs that vow'd chaste life
    to keep
Came tripping by; but in her maiden hand
The fairest votary took up that fire
Which many legions of true hearts had
    warm'd;
And so the general of hot desire
Was sleeping by a virgin hand disarm'd.
This brand she quenched in a cool well by,
Which from Love's fire took heat perpetual,
Growing a bath and healthful remedy
For men diseased; but I, my mistress' thrall,
  Came there for cure, and this by that I
    prove,
  Love's fire heats water, water cools not
    love.